MW01168856

Esther Season: A Devotional Toolkit for Women Walking in Purpose

Spiritual Strategy • Divine Identity • Quiet Power

Welcome

Welcome, Queen. This toolkit is for the woman who knows she is called, chosen, and set apart. Inspired by Queen Esther, this devotional will help you align with divine timing, strategy, and identity.

What is Esther Season?

Esther Season is a time of preparation, elevation, and divine purpose. Like Queen Esther in the Bible, you are being positioned for a moment greater than yourself. This is your season of spiritual growth, quiet strategy, and bold obedience. (Esther 4:14)

How to Use This Toolkit

Use this devotional daily or weekly to reflect, pray, plan, and activate. It's a mix of scripture, journaling, strategy worksheets, and personal empowerment.

7-Day Devotional Warm-Up

Day 1

Scripture: Esther 2:17 - You are chosen

Devotional Reflection:

Personal Prayer:

Esther Move of the Day:

Notes:

Day 2

Scripture: Jeremiah 29:11 - God's plans for you

Devotional Reflection:

Personal Prayer:

Esther Move of the Day:

Notes:

Day 3

Scripture: Proverbs 3:5-6 - Trust and direction

Devotional Reflection:

Personal Prayer:

Esther Move of the Day:

Notes:

Day 4

Scripture: Romans 8:28 - Purpose through process

Devotional Reflection:

Personal Prayer:

Esther Move of the Day:

Notes:

Day 5

Scripture: Psalm 46:5 - God is within her

Devotional Reflection:

Personal Prayer:

Esther Move of the Day:

Notes:

Day 6

Scripture: 2 Timothy 1:7 - Power, love, sound mind

Devotional Reflection:

Personal Prayer:

Esther Move of the Day:

Notes:

Day 7

Scripture: Esther 4:14 - For such a time as this

Devotional Reflection:

Personal Prayer:

Esther Move of the Day:

Notes:

Identity in Royalty

Activity: Who Am I in God's Eyes? (Isaiah 43:1, 1 Peter 2:9)

Affirmation Builder: I am crowned with...

Mirror Work Prompts: Today I will show up as...

Divine Strategy & Quiet Power
Esther Season Devotional Toolkit

Esther didn't just pray—she planned. So do you, Queen.

Spiritual Insight

Scripture/Word of the Day:
Write the scripture or word God has highlighted for you today.

Verse: _____

What it's saying to me:

Divine Assignment

What has God placed on your heart to pursue or steward right now?
Be real—what's heavy, what's clear, what's tugging at your spirit?

Current Reality Check

Where am I now (emotionally, spiritually, financially, mentally)?
Honest, sis. You can't shift what you won't face.

Esther Strategy Session

3 Strategic Moves I Can Make This Week:
(These are your "for such a time as this" moves. Quiet power plays.)

1. _____

2. _____

3. _____

Private Prayers + Power Plays

What am I laying before God in secret today?
This is your war room moment. Pour it out.

🙏 _____

🙏 _____

🙏 _____

Queenly Affirmation

Write a personal affirmation based on what you've reflected on.
(Ex: "I am equipped for divine impact. I do not shrink—I rise.")

👑 _____

👑 _____

Esther Goals Sheet (Habakkuk 2:2)

Esther Goals Sheet

Habakkuk 2:2 — "Write the vision; make it plain on tablets, so he may run who reads it."

Vision Statement

What is the clear, bold vision God has given me for this season?

Goal Breakdown

List your major goals for this season (3–5). Make them specific and measurable.

1. _____

2. _____

3. _____

4. _____

5. _____

Action Steps

For each goal, what 2–3 steps will I take to make it happen?

Goal 1: _____

- **Step 1:** _____

- **Step 2:** _____

- **Step 3:** _____

Goal 2: _____

- **Step 1:** _____

- **Step 2:** _____

- **Step 3:** _____

Goal 3: _____

- **Step 1:** _____

- **Step 2:** _____

- **Step 3:** _____

Goal 4: _____

- **Step 1:** _____

- **Step 2:** _____

- **Step 3:** _____

Goal 5: _____

- **Step 1:** _____

- **Step 2:** _____

- **Step 3:** _____

Progress Tracking

Use this space weekly to track wins and areas to improve.

Week Wins & Progress Challenges & Adjustments Needed Notes/Prayer Requests

1

2

3

4

5

6

7

8

9

10

11

12

Accountability & Support

Who will I call on to keep me accountable? Who supports this vision?
(Name, contact, role)

_____

_____

_____

Prayer for Purpose

Lord, help me to pursue these goals with clarity, courage, and consistency.
Let my vision be clear and my steps ordered by You. Amen.

_____

"For I know the plans I have for you," declares the Lord, "plans to prosper you and not to harm you, plans to give you hope and a future." — **Jeremiah 29:11**

_____

Spiritual Warfare & Confidence

Prayer Strategy Map

"Be strong in the Lord and in His mighty power." — Ephesians 6:10

---

1. Belt of Truth

Prayer Focus: **Stand firm in God's truth.**
Prayer Points:

- Declare God's Word over your life and goals.
- Pray for discernment to recognize lies and distractions.
- Affirm: "I am rooted in truth, and no deception can move me."

---

2. Breastplate of Righteousness

Prayer Focus: **Protect your heart and actions.**
Prayer Points:

- Ask God to guard your heart from negativity and compromise.
- Pray for integrity in all decisions.
- Affirm: "My heart and mind are aligned with God's righteousness."

---

3. Feet Fitted with the Gospel of Peace

Prayer Focus: **Walk in peace and purpose.**
Prayer Points:

- Pray for peace in your journey and clarity in your path.
- Ask for boldness to move forward without fear.
- Affirm: "I walk in peace, ready to spread love and truth."

---

4. Shield of Faith

Prayer Focus: Deflect doubt and fear.
Prayer Points:

- Declare faith over every challenge and obstacle.

- Pray for unwavering trust in God's promises.

- Affirm: "My faith is a shield no fear can penetrate."

---

5. Helmet of Salvation

Prayer Focus: Protect your mind with salvation's hope.
Prayer Points:

- Pray for renewal of your mind daily.

- Ask for clarity and protection from negative thoughts.

- Affirm: "My mind is guarded by the hope of salvation."

---

6. Sword of the Spirit (God's Word)

Prayer Focus: Use God's Word as your offensive weapon.
Prayer Points:

- Memorize and declare Scripture over your life.

- Pray for wisdom to apply God's Word in every situation.

- Affirm: "The Word of God is my sword and guide."

---

7. Pray in the Spirit

Prayer Focus: Stay connected to the Holy Spirit.
Prayer Points:

- Ask for guidance and strength from the Holy Spirit.

- Pray continually for spiritual growth and boldness.

- Affirm: "I am led and empowered by the Holy Spirit."

Reflection & Notes

- How did you feel after this prayer?

- What revelations or peace did you receive?

- What action steps will you take this week?

Armor of God Reflection Pages

Daily Reflection: Armor Piece Focus

1. Belt of Truth

- **What lies or false beliefs do I need to replace with God's truth today?**

- **How can I remind myself to stand firm in truth in my daily life?**

- **Affirmation: "I wear the Belt of Truth, and I walk confidently in God's reality."**

2. Breastplate of Righteousness

- **What areas of my heart need protection right now?**

- **How can I practice righteousness even when it's hard?**

- **Affirmation: "My heart is guarded by righteousness and aligned with God's will."**

3. Feet Fitted with the Gospel of Peace

- Where do I need peace in my life?

- What steps can I take to walk boldly in faith and peace?

- Affirmation: "I walk with peace and purpose, grounded in the Gospel."

---

4. Shield of Faith

- What fears or doubts do I need to cover with faith?

- How will I choose faith over fear today?

- Affirmation: "My faith shields me from doubt and empowers me to move forward."

5. Helmet of Salvation

- **What thoughts do I need to protect or renew today?**

- **How does the hope of salvation influence my mindset?**

- **Affirmation: "My mind is protected and renewed by the hope of salvation."**

6. Sword of the Spirit

- What scripture can I claim as my weapon for today?

- How will I use God's Word to fight spiritual battles this week?

- Affirmation: "God's Word is my sword, guiding and empowering me."

7. Pray in the Spirit

- How am I staying connected to the Holy Spirit?

- What areas do I need the Spirit's guidance and strength?

- Affirmation: "I am led and strengthened by the Holy Spirit daily."

Weekly Reflection

- **Which piece of the armor did I rely on most this week?**

- **What victories or breakthroughs did I experience?**

- **What's one area I want to strengthen next week?**

Notes & Prayer Requests

Declarations & War Room Affirmations

Speak It, Queen! — Daily Declarations

(Powerful, faith-filled statements that set the tone for your day)

- I am fearfully and wonderfully made, equipped for greatness. (Psalm 139:14)

- I walk in purpose and power, no weapon formed against me shall prosper. (Isaiah 54:17)

- I am a daughter of the King, crowned with strength and dignity. (Proverbs 31:25)

- My mind is renewed; I reject every negative thought. (Romans 12:2)

- I am blessed to be a blessing; abundance flows through me. (2 Corinthians 9:8)

- I declare peace over my heart and my home. (John 14:27)

- I rise above every challenge with grace and resilience. (Philippians 4:13)

War Room Affirmations

(Powerful one-liners to say aloud, lock in your faith, and push through the battles)

- I am protected by the armor of God.

- My faith is bigger than my fears.

- I claim victory in every area of my life.

- I speak life, not death, over my dreams.

- Divine favor surrounds me like a shield.

- I rest in God's timing and trust His plan.

- I am unstoppable, unshakable, and unbreakable.

Your Personal Power Play

- **What's your main affirmation or declaration?**

_____

- **How will you embody this truth in your actions?**

_____

- **Prayer focus:**

_____

_____

Write Your Own Decree

Date: _____

_____

Speak Your Truth, Queen

This is your moment to declare what your heart is believing, what your spirit is commanding. Write your own powerful decree below — bold, clear, and rooted in your purpose and faith.

_____

My Personal Decree:
I decree that...

_____

_____

_____

_____

_____

Scripture or Affirmation I Stand On:

_____

_____

_____

Why This Decree Matters to Me:

_____

_____

_____

_____

Action Steps to Bring This Decree to Life:

1. _____

2. _____

3. _____

_____

Prayer to Seal My Decree:
(Write a short prayer to confirm and invite divine alignment)

_____

_____

_____

_____

Bonus Section: Love, Sisterhood & Legacy

Letter to Your Younger Self

A Letter to Another Esther

Legacy Intention Sheet

Date: _____

What Legacy Do I Want to Leave?

(Think beyond yourself — how do you want to be remembered?)

_____

_____

_____

Values I Want to Pass On

(What core beliefs and principles will guide my legacy?)

_____

_____

_____

Impact I Want to Create

(Who will benefit from my work, love, and leadership?)

_____

_____

_____

Actions I Commit to Taking Today

(What daily steps align with my legacy vision?)

1. _____

2. _____

3. _____

Prayer or Affirmation for My Legacy

(Invite divine guidance to empower your legacy journey)

Final Prayer: I Was Made For This

God,

I come before You knowing that I was made for this moment, this purpose, this

season.

I was not an accident, nor a mistake—

I am fearfully and wonderfully made, crafted with intention and love.

Give me the strength when I feel weak,

the clarity when I feel confused,

and the courage to walk boldly in the path You have set for me.

Help me to trust Your timing and embrace my unique gifts.

Let my light shine so bright that it cannot be ignored,

and may my impact ripple through generations.

I release doubt, fear, and distraction—

replacing them with faith, focus, and fierce determination.

I was made for this.

I am ready. I am worthy.

I am equipped.

In Your name, I declare victory.

Amen.

Made in the USA
Columbia, SC
09 July 2025

60532123R00022